SEEKING AND FINDING THE ONE

SEEKING AND FINDING THE ONE

Sadhika M

COPYRIGHT

Title: Seeking and Finding the One
Author: Sadhika M (Penymous)
Cover Design: Sadhika M (Penymous)
Interior Design: Sadhika M (Penymous)
Publisher: Journey Press
Copyright: 2023
ISBN: 978-0-692-06834-2
1.Spirituality 2.Poetry 3.Hinduism 4.Metaphysical

Permission is hereby granted to copy any part of this book for personal use. Written request must be made to use or quote in public and/or commercial ventures, and written permission of the author must be displayed in such use. Requests for such use may be made in writing to the author, care of Journey Press, 2132 Conway Road, Ashfield, MA 01330.

The Isha Upanishad, a sacred text from India, begins with an invocation, which, roughly translated, says "That (i.e. the Divine) is full and complete. This (i.e. the created world) is full and complete, because what springs from the complete is complete, and after giving birthto the complete, the source remains full and complete."

The Sanskrit word for this fullness is "purna". It also means prefection. Hence, the Upanishads is declaring that the peace, freedom from fear, contentment and joy that are the perfection of life we yearn for, is resting in the fullness of one's own nature. It is speaking of a holiness that is wholeness. It is telling us that we *are* the Divine, in the same way that rays of the sun are not different from the sun, flames are the same as the fire, and a handful of water from the ocean is of the same substance as the ocean. At the same time, the sun-ray longs to return to the radiant One that it shone out from; the flame sinks back into the fire, and the handful of water wants to be free from the hand that separated it from the ocean. As long as we are embodied, we live in the paradox of separation-in-oneness.

The journey to the One is often confusing and full of longing, reversals, and rabbit trails. We are trying to peel off limiting belief structures that have become our reality, so we are walking blind. These seem so real that someone once said, "Trying to do this on one's own is like trying to jump over one's own head." Sometimes we sense the "purna", but either we cannot reach it or we cannot stay in it. We need guides, just as we need teachers to develop a skill or learn to live in society.

Words are not enough to offer gratitude to those who have been my guides on this path to the God who is my source and my own substance. Sw. Ramananda (1916-1952), who first awakened me to the reality of a path to the Divine, Sw. Nityananda (1898-1961), who taught me that the Divine is within, and my living teacher Sri M (1948-), who helped me peel off more false beliefs in the past eight months than I managed to do in forty years: May I always bow to you in loving reverence.

Sadhika

CONTENTS

THE BACKSTORY — 1

SEEKING

Colors-gazing Woman	4
Forget It, Ma!	5
Coyote	6
Crazy Woman	7
Eye of I	8
Rage	9
I Got Nuthin'	10
More and More and More of You	11
Dawn Prayer	12
Eulogy or Awakening	15
No Way!	17
Unborn	18
Upside Down and Sideways	19
You Write This Poem with My Blood	20
Being There	22
Stillness at the End	23
Delight!	24

AND FINDING

Little Resurrected Girl	26
Did You Just Burn Down My House?	27
Everyday Magic	28
Nityananda	29
Yes, We Play	30
After the Storm	31
All	32

Kali's Songs of Change	33
Becoming Human	34
Celebrant	35
Breath Circles Time	36
Spider Woman	37
Merging	38
God Wounds Quietly	39
Mike	40
Who Is There?	41
My Tribe	42
Silence Comes in Flavors	43
The Seed Sound	44
The One at the Center	45
Waking Dreams	46
Open Book with Blank Pages	47
Anami	48

THE ONE

You Enchantress!	50
Holy Mother, Sacred Child	51
Full	54
Deathless Body	55
Blue	56
Empty to the Brim	57
Divine Beauty	58
Core	59
Freedom is Scary, Kali Ma	60
Kali's Eyes	61
Kyrie	62

Mary Full of Grace	63
Wild Mary	64
Passion of Kali	65
An Offering to Maha-Lakshmi	67
Rain Dancer	68
Snow Bird	69
Rage and Ecstasy in My Heart	70
What Self?	72
ABOUT THE AUTHOR	73

THE BACK STORY

These poems are snapshots of my journey into the One that began when I was twenty-six. One evening, out of the blue, I encountered the One. It (He, She) came as infinite consciousness-energy, an unimaginable radiance made of a power that was also love. It was itself, and it was me. Consciousness-energy is conscious. It is aware of itself and others, and it communicates - in short, a being. Hence, my experience of Spirit started as a relationship with an Infinite Person.

  The experience lasted only a minute or two, because my body could not have survived the influx of energy. I never again experienced the Beloved in its full presence, but the glimmers I have had of Her/Him sometimes spilled over into words that became poems. Some of them are in this small collection.

  At times I call the Divine "Mother", because it is the source from which I bubble up moment by moment. The Divine is also my lover: The Infinite Person was made of all the ways that one can love another – the way a child loves its parent, the way a mother or a father loves her/his child, the way one can love a precious friend. When these different threads of love are woven into one cloth, as they were in the Being I encountered, the love between lover and beloved comes closest to the ecstasy that is God's substance. At least that is my experience.

In these poems, the Divine is India's goddess Kali of the battlefield as well as Mary. He is the lover who abandoned me, and the guy who works at a slaughterhouse. God is a bird hopping on the snow, the dance of rain, and my own self. In my experience, Divine being infuses all forms as their essence. S/He is also pure consciousness beyond all forms, and has no form at all that defines Her. All forms are Her form; all faces are faces of Her energy. And... nothing is Her form because we can experience but cannot exhaust the infinite through experience. That is why these poems are simply evanescent snapshots of the ceaseless divine flow that makes up our world of form and experience.

I organized the poems into three sections, titled "Seeking", "And Finding", and "The One". They reflect the three primary movements in my journey. The language is simple and direct as is my experience. I tried to guide the rhythm of reading by capitalizing the first word of a line or leaving it in lowercase. Where you encounter a line that is a continuation of a sentence but the first word is capitalized, pause for a fraction of a second. Then you will know me a little better and share something of my journey.

Sadhika

SEEKING

COLORS-GAZING WOMAN

SOME CALL YOU "SHYAMA", the Blue One
but You've always come to me
wearing the colors of love
Colors of dawn
Color of longing
Color of the silver growing in my hair
as I still wait for you.
As the color of tears
year after year missing You
As the rainbow colors of finding You
Color of the mist hiding You.
Color of just noticing
neither seeking nor finding.
Color of remembrance
Helplessness
And hope
In my wide-open staring eyes.

In India, divine forms are often depicted as having blue skin, echoing the "Blue Person" in the visions of the 12th Century Christian mystic Hildegard of Bingen. Why blue, I have no idea. No one does.

FORGET IT, MA!

"WHITE PURITY!" you command of me!
No, Mother.
I bring you my rainbow colors.
They bloomed from a faint flicker of soul
That opened its eyes and whispered
in naive wonder at a fresh new world,
 "Mother".
I bring You my blossoming
from that tentative flicker
from that one-dimensional purity like white-wash
Into a queen,
And a witch,
A giant maple and a trash heap.
All of my riches, all of my slime.
I bring You my rainbow life.
You want white purity from all this, Mother?
Knead itYourself, for I do not know how.
Join me in my rainbow life, for
without You my rainbow would fade
into the muddy despairing flat mundane
Where hope drowns without even a sigh.

COYOTE

AS DAY AND NIGHT EMBRACE
spreading across the sky
Night turns gently
Covering her lover's body with her own
Stirring a deeper knowing, letting
long-forgotten senses awake.
Twin hearts we are, me and the Gray One
as wisps of Peace soak us in silence.
Her glistening form is a dream
in the slithering mist.
The mist covers the Gray One
and the Gray One
breathes the mist.

For a moment we are the Silence
that holds the Mystery.

Then I turn toward my world
Of head lights, wet streets, and square buildings
The Gray One just behind my eyes,
Just behind my breath
For a precious while of re-membering.

CRAZY WOMAN

I MET HER ONCE ON THE subway in New York.
I was twenty-four
She was old and bald
And talked to herself.
Sacred woman unredeemed
For no one dared look with their naked eyes.
I ache for her.
Sick fear uncoils from my belly, and rises -
An icy electric fire -
into my brain.
My face flows into hers
in the sacrifice of redemption.
I remember
the eyes around us tunneling into the abyss
Refusing the sacrifice.
Looking into the wounded gloom in the human soul
I am sweaty
Trying to not fall in.

EYE OF I

WHOSE FACE IS THIS ill-fitting face that I am wearing?
The wasp stings with all its coiled killer energy
and accepts death as part of the flow.
The wild geese caw
holding nothing back.
The saint dives into his supper
honestly famished, slurps with unconditioned joy.
They live in their true faces.

Behind this shiny, pink-cheeked, red-lipped mask
I keep on chiseling
with a line from this face and a line from that -
because *one* must be mine! -
is an "I" that the eye cannot see
A Being that need not become,
An empty cavern
Filled
with a wind that is
laden with faces if you want one,
A wind that is solid bliss
if you let it be.

RAGE

IN THE RAVENOUS NIGHT my feet lost the ground
Slammed by the blood lust of
inchoate voices of dark things
Rising from their hidden dungeon inside me.
They drew blood from the soft green maiden spirit
in rage-clenched jaws.
They fell back, shrieking helplessly
when from the blood emerged
Mother, with incomparable majesty.

The Mother knows the smell and taste of blood
from Her loins birthing life
and Her sword slashing what must go
Protecting even dark things
made ugly in their cauldron of pain.

Their pain withered the Mother's beauty
into the spare lines of the Crone.
Now her wizened old fingers
pry open a rusty old wound groaning in rebellion.
The Crone heals with mercy
And no pity.

I GOT NUTHIN'

I HAVE A CHILD'S SWORD in my hand
Made of wood.
It doesn't cut anything.
That is my will.
My lamp is guttering
Because I wasted the oil
looking at painted-on sparkle
hiding tarnish beneath.
I never built a damn in my life
and now I can't dam up my passion to reach You
but watch it wash away each day.

And whose fault is this, Mother,
if, as they say, Your will is supreme?

MORE AND MORE AND MORE OF YOU

I SAW YOU TONIGHT PEEKING between the trees
And in moon shadows on the snow.
For one moment
Your beauty crowded out the stark winter night
as beginnings crowd endings in the summer garden.
Your beauty sank into my heart
like honeyed gold
And glows there now, warm and rich
Maddening.
You are here and not here
because I can't help it –
I want more, and more, and more of You.
Desire is on the right path but gives up too soon:
Less than All can never satisfy.

DAWN PRAYER

THE FIRST STREAKS OF light
are ripping open the silky night air
draped around the hills,
Wrapped around me,
Like a cocoon of black nothingness.
Cold air pushes darkly against my breath –
A last struggle of night.
But the birds are already dreaming dreams of warmth
and suddenly
Hope spreads like a wildfire of bird song everywhere.
The coals I lit are glowing under a feathering of ash.
The shimmering air over the brazier
is expecting my prayer now.

The earth gave me rice.
I offer it back to the rising fire and watch
as new smoke, sacred with rice-essence
Carries my prayer up to the Gods.

The earth fed me with wheat.
Placing a grain carefully on the coals
I remember
how satisfying, the wheat
to my pulsing, reaching blood.

Dark perfumes from spongy forest floors,
sun-lit smells of just-cut grass,
sweat trickling hot down my breasts in August,
metallic tastes in the snow-bearing air...

SEEKING AND FINDING THE ONE

All etched a thousand soul memories into my bones.
A drop of precious rose oil is sizzling now in the brazier:
An offering of thanks
for all those precious drops of time.

I offer milk, in thanks for the lives being born today
And sage, in gratitude for the mountains
who will remember me for a long time.

Lifting my hands in prayer,
Streams of light sweep across the universe.
Breathing in,
liquid gold drowns all thought in radiance.
The coals, now in my heart
Fanned by each breath
shimmer into blinding light.
Light is humming but I cannot hear.
Straining to listen,
the body surrenders her boundary
and melts
Quietly
Into the infinite.
Where I was,
Limitless, roiling waves of Light.
Boiling, infinite waves of Light
curling on Light, leaping on Light, upon
rushing streams of Light
Alone.

Tears streaming down to my chin
In rivulets

SADHIKA M.

Shiver me awake.
Greeting the sun
I am ready to begin the day.

EULOGY OR AWAKENING

YOU COULD SINK ENDLESSLY into the
dark, sucking pool of grief in her brown eyes.
A pain too raw to feel
sometimes peered out between her sparse lashes
into a world that crushed her mercilessly, and
she starved
For lack of one drop of kindness
that would green the field of dust that was her life
as out of her heart leaked a young girl's dreams turned to
vinegar in her airless breast.
They were nectar once, promises
poured into her soul drop by drop by divine fingers.
Why did God's soft fingertips then wound her like
tiger's claws she did not ask.
She was born behind veils –
The black veil that hid the sunlight from her mother's face
The lattice-veil that made her windows
a "No" that would not open
The veil that kept her heart cocooned with its dreams
until it was torn from her on her wedding night and
she was thrust, naked, into a world waiting for her
with a thousand knives.
She unlocked the crypt of her heart when she let me
fly into my freedom, and
closed the door behind her in her silent cave
Where she died quietly,
As she had lived.

She was my mother.
Her name was Seniha.

SADHIKA M.

The weight, the weight, the crushing weight
of these words drag me to the depths where
her captive soul floats
unsaved.
I hold her, tight,
My strong legs kicking up, up, up
Towards radiance
Towards sunlight
Salt air
And my own deliverance.

NO WAY!

WORTHY. UNWORTHY.
Two pieces of camphor over a flame,
They melt into one fragrant smoke
curling out to ... where?
The vastness absorbs.
It doesn't really care or know
about two or one.

The Way is all there is
And when there is no not-Way
there is no Way.
We live in the center of this rose like
trapped bees inside a flower that closed around them
drunk on the fragrance seeping into our buzzing, hallucinating
gold and silver in the fog and
fangs hidin in leaves in the trees and
stench blowing in the morning breeze
and honey in a swamp.
Truth is,
This rose is the womb of the universe
Redolent with perfumes of longing
Perfumes of Love
Of seeking, finding,
Of remembering....
Perfume of....
Whatever you want to dream.

UNBORN

SHE STANDS PARALYZED BEFORE the ever-now
Seared by the clear light of oneness
No longer knowing how to skip rope
between the past and the future.
She cannot grieve, or hope, or fear.
She stares, unblinking, into a radiance
That is the first cause,
The essence,
And the funeral pyre
Of every created thing.
This radiance cannot be seen
but blesses through eyes that forgot how to blink.
The final and terrible simplicity
of freedom.

UPSIDE DOWN AND SIDEWAYS

SAY YOU MEET SOMEONE
Who is starving for more hunger.
What would fill his belly?
Suppose somebody else grabbed your arm
craving thirst, parched for more thirst.
What would quench her mounting fire?
If another one came, searching sleeplessly for sleep
How would you give her rest?

One who is in love with Love
swam out to measure that ocean
and drowned into her becoming.

It is said, "Love is the Becoming of Being"
And the One is turning that one back into One.

SADHIKA M.

YOU WRITE THIS POEM WITH MY BLOOD

WORDS CHOKE
in this upsurge,
This primal howl
This tsunami of yearning
that cannot surge quite high enough
to join Your shoreless ecstasy.
My yearning crashes
like a wave that gave up, and
drenches the land
in torrential salty downpourings of despair.
So strange is this tryst with You.
I ache from Your lack when I almost touch You
through that invisible veil -
Of what, I do not know.
The hunter's spear sinks into my heart
just as my fingertips brush Your fragrant ecstasy.
I fear this dance will only end
when I have danced myself to death
turning and turning around You
spiraling smaller and smaller into endless depths
And out onto a horizon that expands without end.

Why do You play this cruel game
Throwing out sparks by the handful
  from Your own heart
and watching them burn
with the longing to return?

I wish I could burn out
Float away

SEEKING AND FINDING THE ONE

A speck of dead gray ash
no longer playing the game.
But I am life eternal and cannot die.

Endless column of Fire -
have You not had enough oblations yet?
Have not enough hearts
ripped themselves open
and poured their longing blood into Your flames?
What kind of veil is this that it glistens with
infinite bliss on one side
And a million bloody tears on the other?
How does this story end?
How does this poem that is my life
find its final line
flowing from Your pen
That writes with my blood?

BEING THERE

MEDITATION IS AN OCEANIC wave
that washes over you
And recedes.
Tonight at low tide I prayed: "Don't leave me."
Words formed like froth
on the receding wave:
"Don't let me leave You.
"Don't let me veil You behind a flickering mind."
Now I pray to my mind,
Not to God.
God already wants me.
It is my mind that could not care less.

STILLNESS AT THE END

YOU ARE MY BEGINNING and my end.
Outside of time,
Taking no space,
End joins Beginning in Your Zen brush
painting the circle of time,
The land of Kala*,
the Dancing Kali.
My beginning is Your dance
as You kick up galaxies and
churn Being into Becoming;
my end is the silence of One -
The roar of Your first explosion into form
fading to the hum of creation "AUM",
absorbed, finally, into whatever remains
when Your dance fades away.

You are my beginning and my end.
The circle is almost full
Your brush almost dry....
I wait for the last few black streaks to fade
as End joins Beginning
outside the realm of time.

Kala: the flow of time. Everything goes down before the flow of time and the flow of change In it. Kali is the mistrss of time, of the ever-flowing change that gives life to each form and every experience - only once and only for a while. Nothing remains or repeats in the realm of Kali. However, Kali is not barren destruction. She is the source of ever-new creation. Dare to enter into Her consciousness and you will find the eternal spirit that exists in the Now, outside the realm of time.

DELIGHT!

A SINGLE ATOM OF DELIGHT is this uni-multiverse.
That is Allah; that is Rahim; that is Shiva; that is Rām.
The delight trembling each thing alive is That.
The delight that quickens as desire is That.
The delight in the first thrill of possessing is That.

Crack open the shell
Unhook delight from the object that snared it.
Trace the shimmering thread of delight with
all you've got inside and more,
Deeper and deeper into your soil
Into your soul.
Follow that root seeking groundwaters deep inside
all the way back to That -
To the causeless, objectless, innocent delight
that knows itself inside your own body
that is God.

AND FINDING

LITTLE RESURRECTED GIRL

ONCE UPON A TIME I lived in the "Bright"
And the "Bright" lived in me.
A living cord of "Bright"
made me playmate to all that is.
The pine forest flowed emerald green in the "Bright"
and the forest seeped into me.
The life of my street glowed in the "Bright"
and a river of life poured into me.
The fresh light of the market sparkled in the "Bright"
 and a bright joy sparkled inside of me.

A liquid Light, pure Grace,
an unadorned suchness flowed today.
Its brightness seeped into me
and I flowed into the "Bright" on the same cresting wave.
The living "Bright" is all there is,
it trickles from my pores and out into
the seven directions today.
Its light comes home to rest
in Your sacred peace, my Bhagavan
And I lay in the lap of Your living silence
my grateful, now white-haired head.

Seven Directions: The 4 cardinal points plus Out Into the Universe, In towards the Center, and the ineffable direction that is everywhere. From a Mohawk tradition.

Bhagavan means "divine" in Sanskrit. It is an adjective often placed before the name of a respected sage or a mythical divine being.

DID YOU JUST BURN DOWN MY HOUSE?

YOU BLOW LIKE A TEMPEST,
Wrenching my life loose from its grooves,
My Divine Mother.
And you burn my house down
Because it is small and dark,
And tired.
Sitting in the holy flame You lit
My bones, my blood, my cells
dance faster than they can, really.
I burn up.
But who cares, my mother Kali?
Who needs a body when you adorn me with a universe
of myriad names and forms?
Who needs a lid shutting my mind
when I can get soaking wet under infinite skies pouring
a monsoon of Grace?
Who needs a God all sugar and spice and everything nice
when
Truth growls with bared bloody fangs every day?
I need a holiness that is wholeness, mother Kali.
a heart solidly planted in these shifting sands,
in the terrible beauty of death, rot, birth, life
aah! Again! Aah! Again!
I seek the Grace of change we cannot bargain with
in your maelstrom of dance.
The dance is never the same
The dancer never changes.
Those who seek only the dancer should remember:
She is, only because of Her crazy dance.

EVERYDAY MAGIC

WET SOUNDS OF A RAINY day.
Curled-up leaves staggering under the leaden sky.
Inside, wood burning, warmth;
My home feels so cozy.
Sipping the strong, sweet tea
the soft animal of my body grows quiet.
It is safe to
let the Infinite in.

NITYANANDA

MAKING TEA IS A wave rising, falling
in the still space of One
that is Nityānanda.
Sipping the breath in meditation
is the silent ecstasy of Nityānanda.
Folding, curving, melting silently
into its own being
is the glittering joy of Nityānanda.
The stillness where the out-breath turns back in,
is the inward gaze of Nityānanda.
The cave where
thoughts meld with rapture-light
in one blinding intensity
is the seat of Nityānanda.
The beginningless silence of the All-Light
is the unborn sound of Nityānanda.
As you give up your very being into the unheard sound,
You enter into Nityānanda.

Nityananda means unwavering peace and joy. It is also the popular name by which a great sage of India, who lived in the first half of the twentieth century, was known. No one knew his real name, so the people began to call him Nityananda, in acknowledgment of his unchanging state of bliss.

YES, WE PLAY

Oh, man! I am lost
in a wild, uncontrolled sort of joy.
I am looking for a sign: "You are here";
Some landmark, please, so I can carve my mind into
 this versus that and here as in "not there",
So I can capture the joy soaking the ground of all
under barbed wire scaffolds of
Definition. Reason. Cause. Effect.

Thank God
this joy is a living thing, and
way more nimble than me.
It laughs its escape
Doesn't let me crush it under my knees
bent in prayer
On spine-crushing all-night vigils on a cold floor.
It tells me it is sprinkling living green into my sleep
Thrilling the nucleus of my
every cell with its laughter, and
rippling us out further into mists of mischievous joy.
It just is.
I just am.
I am.

AFTER THE STORM

THE STORM SURGES CEASED.
Longing no longer hurls itself,
A bone-crushing battering ram
against a door that will not open.
Bowing before You Are - I Am
Longing emptied into a lake of surrender.
On its surface a joy plays now, delicate as a
butterfly fresh from its cocoon.
All the dazzling colors that intoxicated the inner eye
gave way to a crystalline something.
The symphony inside gave in
to a single note on a single flute.
I know You are / I Am.
I know like the mountains know
Like the birds and the angels,
Like You know.
My face a child again,
I know I reached my Beloved's door.

ALL

A FIELD OF SPARKLING DROPS
Extending as far as the eye can see...
God-drops... Creation...
The exquisite surface of spirit we call "form".
My breath is one with the Beautiful One
Where He and I offer our all
Into each other.

"Come", twinkle the sounds of His anklets jingling
As He dances this world-play
"Sweep away that shaky boundary
Where your skin touches the air.
Let your skin be air, and the air your body,
your breath Me in you, and
you a ripple in My dance.
Let go! To where all is your self
All is your body and nobody."

KALI'S SONGS OF CHANGE

THE SOUNDS OF ENDINGS
pierce the stillness creeping over the hills.
A last birdsong, a hunter's gun, chainsaw in the forest....
With needle-edged sounds
The sharp air of autumn touches me.
A leaf flutters to the ground
Brushing from inside, my heart.
I shiver, walking the razor's edge between
letting go and wakefulness
With sure footing.

LATE WINTER.
Snow falling like lace
Into the still space between trees.
With tiny sparkling sounds
Snow kisses their silence
Smell of life
Already stirring in their dreams.

BECOMING HUMAN

I. ME. MINE. YOU.
HeSheTheyYours.
Walls trembling in terror
where that holy rascal hiding inside you
toppled a boulder of
Refusal
that would not allow.

Boundaries to patrol with vigilance
Or if we fail – please, God, no!- they will be breached
in the onslaught of the zombie mob's insatiable need....

How did life turn from liquid light-with-no-end into
such jagged blocks of ice-cold fear?

No point to this imaginary line, this individuality
All reverence, all joy to this unique line on God's face
called my personality.
You teach me today how to be human, my heart:
To be nothing
And everything
And to be one beautiful line
on the blindingly beautiful face of Light.

CELEBRANT

SUNLIGHT CANNOT REACH these depths.
The depths know stillness
Sunlight knows the dance.
The reed plays their songs to each other.
The body can sing this song of two notes, too:
Mineral into bark into flesh into breath into light
Light into life into flesh into death into rot
And transformation.
Your body is a reed
But no music can play through
If your spirit is stuffed into it
and sealed in at both ends.

Breathe into silence once and empty yourself.
Listen to the sound sunlight makes
skipping on the water
Rippling on grasses like a harp
and phrasing cadences in clouds.
Listen to the deep droning beneath
and overtones reaching into blue infinity.
You can sing their songs to each other,
Celebrant of this Holy Mass,
You can unite the earth and stars.
Just listen!

BREATH CIRCLES TIME

AT THE EDGE OF SPACE
Earth and Sky blend.
The rivers flow into Time
And Time
Into Timelessness.
"Now" is infinite
Stirless in all directions
But for the imperceptible wave of breath
Keeping rhythm
Keeping time.
In-breath opening into Space,
Out-breath pouring into Eternity
And in the circle of time in between
I am.
Arched across the spaceless gate
Where ten thousand things rise into form
and sink into nothingness again
To rest
in an unbroken circle.

SPIDER WOMAN

A GOSSAMER WEB BREATHES.
A Woman
is breathing all creatures
Intimately.
A form shimmers into being
where two strands float onto each other
Forming the web on Her breath wind
Delicate as the brush
of a butterfly wing.
A conscious heart,
Brushed,
Quivers in reverence and
touches the earth.

Two strands dance apart
on the Woman's breath wind.
The shimmering stills
The eyes no more,
Closed to the great explosion.
The heart is awake.
Light upon Light again.

Spider Woman is an image of the Creator in several Native American mythologies. It is said that Spider Woman weaves the web of Creation from Her own substance, much like India's Kali and Aditi. My teacher, who was the holder of a Mohawk Learning Way, used to say that wherever two strands meet, there is an individuation - us.

MERGING

EFFERVESCENT DROPS from another world...
Like the first tentative drops of rain
Barely noticed.
Feather-light they land on my skin
and break open into
a lightness of being.
Growing into a deluge
A column of Holy silently descending
Lightens my skin's boundary
into pure awareness so simple
it becomes unbounded Light.
Divine Light, unknown.
Unrecognized Light that casts no shadows
when no one is in the field to know.

Then She sets me down, gently,
Back into this morning,
This place, this body and mind.
Then I know
Where I have been.

GOD WOUNDS QUIETLY

DAWN-BIRD'S CALL pierced
straight into my core.
The rain keeps pattering, softening
the edges of a sepia-colored world
like the faded photographs under
yellowed lace in grandmother's chest.
The bird cried
"Let go of wanting
Of wanting even God
And watch a lake of joy rise quietly
from your pierced core.
I pecked a hole right through you
So Life can flow on His breath
singing 'Huu'."

God wounds to get your attention
That She is, that He is
Already here.

In sufism, "Huu" is the cosmic sound and the divine breath blowing the seeds of Creation through the universe.

MIKE

HE GETS UP AT DAWN like a good yogi.
Every day at 7:00, he goes to the slaughterhouse.
Mike opens the gate at 7:00.
At 8:00 he begins to receive animals –
A parade of innocents Going into the maw of Kali Ma.
He pets them as they come
He fills their water and hay
grief wrapping him tighly
soul to soul with them, until
they each walk that sloping corridor
to that final door, alone but
a ribbon of grief tying his soul to theirs.
Mike practices for 7 hours each day
this sublime spiritual practice
of opening his heart to the suffering of beings.
Mike smiles at you with all his heart
Unconcerned about his two missing front teeth.

WHO IS THERE?

IN THIS SHRINE TO LOVE the entrance is a mirror.
No one has travelled this way for centuries.
The road is thick with dust.
The mirror is blind with dust.
You are blind with the rest of it.
As empty eyes stare barrenly
like dust-choked wells in the desert
someone calls "Who is there?"
"I am" you say, and
a terrific wind swirls up
Casts you back to where you came from.
You journey again, on your knees this time
This time not so sure
a little shy, a little hopeful -
the flickering beginnings of reverence.
"Who is there?" the voice says and you are silent.
You just clean the dust from the mirror
It's the right thing to do
and find yourself held,
Paralyzed,
By the eyes of Love looking at you.
Love looking at Love, the mirror a thinly shimmering line
If the mirror shatters from the intensity,
If the line disappears, then
what becomes of Love looking at Love?

MY TRIBE

BREEZE, MY BUDDY
Welcome to this morning.
I just met a twiglet with two leaves.
It landed on my table
twittering, "Top o' the mornin' to you!"
The bees buzzing importantly
in and out of blooms
An airplane humming - a dot gliding way up in the blue
They are weaving a duet across the sky
just for this morning,
Ephemeral, haunting in its beauty.
My neighbor's hen lost a chick around sunrise.
A fox somewhere is happy – she just fed her child.
My tribe - bee, breeze, twiglet, plane, birth and death
Fold all this richness into one pulsing dome above
that has no rim
other than my consciousness.
What I see, hear, feel,
Is what God sees, hears, feels
of Her limitless life
flowing through the lens of "me".
Who knew? God needs me to see Herself
To know who She is.

SILENCE COMES IN FLAVORS

THERE IS A WHOLE GALLERY of silences
in the sky of mind.
There you can taste
bracing silences
like the moment between a twig snapping in snow
and the sharp in-breath of noticing.
Silences that curve in on themselves
to where the mind cannot follow
Soft lavender silences into which you can
let go all that you are holding.
There are birthing silences
Like the moment when all bird song stops
in praise of sunrise.
There are silences that cloak the heart
in colored silks of dusk
as the sun dissolves in sinking.

I became a connoisseur of silences
and found they had no room to carve up some space for me.
"I" was a thought passing by
In the Great Silence.

THE SEED SOUND

WHEN THOUGHT WINDS stop whistling
another sound rises
like a wind that fills the universe
yet somehow still as soul.
Felt and not heard
it rushes through your cells,
in the spaces between your cells,
sweeping all thinking into a feeling
that is pregnant with All
and about to birth forth.
You swell with the intensity of this sound
from the oceanic womb of creation
and burst forth gratefully on the crashing wave.
You return to the life you know on shore
freshly bathed,
like a child whose eyes
reflect a sparkling world, fresh as dawn,
knowing all there is nothing to know.

THE ONE AT THE CENTER

I tried.
I tried to ascend through the empty sky to safety in Him
to fall again and again
wings beating madly all the way.
I folded my wings and went into free fall
to – I thought – the cave of lost souls.
I fell
Burning
Into a crevasse between iron cliffs of "Will" and "Try!"
I landed in His heart.

Ask me "Is He within or without?", and
I would close my eyes and drift away to Him.
You think "or" has a place in love?
If you ask me, "Is He infinite, great, majestic?"
I would not know – we are too intimate for all that.
If you ask me His name, I would look at you like a deaf-mute.
There are no names at the center.

Call to Him with any name you like – what does it matter?
The Name is a stout rope to hold on to your longing
Until
Exhausted
You free fall.
Then you can even let go of *your* name
in that skin-to-skin embrace
Where lightning flashes from each tiny hair
melt away the hard steel of "you" and "I".
There lovers melt into the gold we all long for
As the world pities the one who has lost her wits.

WAKING DREAMS

EVERY SUNSET GLARES at me with mute accusation
that one more day dissolved behind me.
Heart beat by heart beat She reminds me
Breath by breath I forget.
Night is colder
when my soul helplessly remembers
the warmth of mid-day.
It is said, "Your helplessness and need *are* the way."
Like the sneaking edge of hunger
gnawing its way through the mists of sleep
until you awake,
To say "Hey! I am starving!"
And instantly realize
you were hungry in a dream.

OPEN BOOK WITH BLANK PAGES

The crow's caw sounds like "Maa"
The wind blows "You, You, Youuu"
Form sings love songs to the Formless.
Drops of condensed Radiance look
unknowingly for the sea spray they came from.
Such mercy, that
Radiance gives up its light until we love enough
to seek the Face behind every face, until we ask,
"what is this warm, pulsating life that lies
deeper than the earth's core
yet surrenders to my gaze its mystery?
Could this ever, possibly be
the same glow beating as my heart?"

ANĀMI

WHETHER I COME, or go, or stay, or die,
these things are so ordinary now.
Everything sinks into pure Being filling the sky of Heart.
Finer than a thread of saffron,
purer than spun gold,
This tiny omega point fills entire universes.
This, just a grain of Your Presence, is all I can bear.
Only You can see Yourself.
This, Your beauty, beckons from everywhere and
changes what it sees into Itself.
In the end, it is You, and You, and
You alone
And the eye that tried to see is nowhere to be seen.

Anami means nameless, that is, a divine encounter beyond the mind, hence beyond the faculty of naming.

YOU ENCHANTRESS!

GREAT SPIRIT, CREATRIX,
You are an enchantress.
Your hall of mirrors turns everything topsy-turvy and
we mistake desire for fulfillment
Restlessness for joy
And run around looking for stillness.
Such is Your ceaseless whirling
where You kick up stars and galaxies
As Your mighty feet beat the trance beat of Time.
Then one day
Who knows why or when
The mirrors shatter.
A soul somewhere
awakens
to Your formless radiance sparkling
against a black velvet sky.
Your Name is the incantation that lets it hold on
to the unmoving column,
the light-axis of this mad whirling—
The eternal One
Meditating on Your own true beauty
as the all.

HOLY MOTHER, SACRED CHILD

COME.
Find My secret places
With your touch
Your smell
and your taste buds
quivering alive.

Press your face to my living body
and smell my hidden odors
Of earth, loam, and wild musk
from muscle, sinew, fur
Dancing in ecstasy
My heady dance
of existing.
Smell again
the pine sap, and
green things breathing emerald fresh
on milk I make
from decay, rot, and ooze
richly mixing in my cauldron of death and life
deep beneath this forest floor.
Taste Me now.
Taste My juices
Pungent and tangy in the bitter acorn
tightly guarding its promise,
And my red berry
bursting in grateful release

SADHIKA M.

As you knead
And squeeze
And roll it on your tongue
Honoring the nipple you faintly remember.
Run your fingers through My tangled hair
of these dried branches
tangling your path.
Wild is the hair of Kali they say,
Spreading across earth and sky
As She roars Her wild laughter
of jubilant satiation.
Do you feel gooseflesh
sweeping over your hairs
as Love cascades over your fingers, my child?
It is not mere wind
across the grass and ferns.

Curl up and sleep awhile, my child,
In this nest of crackling oaken leaves
Warm and dry
And I will rock you to the rhythm of being
pulsing in your blood
Your breath
Your flesh
Every cell opening and closing
to My heart beat
pounding the drumbeat of this Great Dance
As I meditate
Immovably
On the pulse of mountains
Cornfields
Waters

SEEKING AND FINDING THE ONE

Forestlands
And you.

Soften now, my child
and let Me open your senses
to the edge of infinity
Where the body knows a reverence
that brings each hair tip alive.
Because I live by this love-making
And you
Can only live in me,
My child.

FULL

ALL THAT I HAVE EVER KNOWN
ever dreamed or desired, is resting
Suspended
in this dome of stillness.
Yet all is moving in this reverberating silent hum.
There is something like a body
Some place throbbing a warmth of gratitude
Swelling, pulsing, beating: my heart.
My mind is clean out of words, seduced by
the pulsation of love that is the face of this silence.
This pulsation curls into itself,
into the secret blue seed of the universe
and back out to the curve of
the cheek of Truth we call form.
This is the pulse of Her life that knows itself
Knows itself to be full.

DEATHLESS BODY

SWEET, DEATHLESS body!
Why are you afraid?
When flesh returns to Earth
water returns to the primal Waters
your warmth returns to Fire and
your air to the vastness of Air
You will live in the deathless elements
inside the womb of the Great Mother
inside this endlessly widening spiral of life.
How can you cease to exist, sweet body?
The Earth, the Air, the Fire, the Water return, return
turn, and return
Spinning delicate filaments of life
into ever-new tapestries in
Her delirious waltz of existence.
So dance joyfully, sweet body.
Grow beyond this form.
Become what none of us can yet imagine.
Imagine!

BLUE

IT IS THE BLUE HOUR.
The deep blue light as evening descends
has the hue of mystery.
She is pregnant with the essence of form
Now that form has vanished into Her blue depths.
Her blue dreams weave the next day into being
Textured with the seeking, finding, loving, fearing...
Of creatures
Whispering their dreams
In Her radiant dark mystery.

EMPTY TO THE BRIM

I AM THE CLAY BETWEEN your hands.
Mould me into my perfection.
Like the birds that leave their nest at dawn
and return at days' end, at seeking's end
Bring me safely to my nest
in the sanctuary of Your breast.
Give me that poverty, that need
Where I draw my very breath as alms from You.
Only those who know, know the riches of this poverty
where soul is made empty for Your in-pouring
and bereft of words, made ready for Your Sound.
Across this velvet peace of emptiness
Tune me like a string
that sings at the mere promise of Your breeze
And sings, and sings, and sings
until there is no sound and no string
Save the whisper of Your Breath on the winds, "Huu".

"Hu" is the sound of the divine breath, which is the moment-to-moment creation of the world, in Sufi traditions.

DIVINE BEAUTY

THERE IS A BEAUTY BEYOND the beauty of form
that is just... beauty.
It leaves my mind no place to hang its hat.
For you can see this beauty
Touch it, twine with it in love play
All without form.
This beauty dazzles
before my closed eyes
But with eyes open?
It is shy
It hides behind the form.
It must hide, for absolute beauty
Unveiled
Turns into blinding light
A love that drowns all else
The bliss that made saints dance.
That is why we crave this world of form so much:
We know Who is behind the veil.

CORE

LOVE IS NOT GENTLE.
Look into the center where
the universe is throbbing and you fill with an "I am"
from where love radiates
like ten thousand petals opening from a fragrant core.
The blissful Mother beckons from the center.
Bewitched, you let yourself fall inward.
You pant for breath as love crushes you
into her own essence.
For love allows no separation.
You sense, trembling,
the annihilation approaching you
but you cannot stop drinking in Her fragrance.
With your last thought you understand
why Kali has white teeth like a strand of pearls.
For love crushes all who dare approach
thinking they will enjoy love.
The mother's food is ego.
She enjoys you,
digesting you into the one eternal stream of bliss
leaping on itself, surging on itself
In its own way.

FREEDOM IS SCARY, KALI MA

MA, SPRING IS HERE.
A hundred years from today
Spring will be here again
but not my voice.
Are You supremely generous
or terminally stingy
I cannot tell.
Moment by moment life passes away
and You never give the same moment twice
even though I cried oceans
For a chance to circle back in time.
And you never stop giving moments, new and precious
To do with them as I will.
I am afraid of You as Time, Ma.
Because You create me and devour me ceaselessly.
It's eat or be eaten here, Ma
So I will pitch one last desperate battle
with the Destroyer of Worlds
Chuckling to myself
For I know:
This is a dance pretending to be battle.

KALI'S EYES

YOU KILL YOUR CHILDREN, they say, Mother,
You destroy them.
You do.
You make them into universes
of a million suns of exploding bliss
Rising, falling in the black sparkle of Your endless eyes.

KYRIE

MOTHER OF MERCY, BLESS us.
In Your mercy we rest
Knowing or not.
On Your mercy comes our next breath
Received with thanks or not.
Through Your mercy Earth brings forth fruit
Gathered with gratitude or not.
Your mercy awakens our hearts' longing for Truth
Its yearning known or not.
Through Your mercy our hearts receive
your holy seed of Light,
Tended with care or not.
In Your mercy we become Light
Willing or not.
Kyrie Eleison.
God's unfathomable mercy
Grace and mercy without measure.

MARY FULL OF GRACE

IN THE DEEP SILENCE OF these early hours
Creation is chanting Your Name, Mother:
"Hail Mary, Mother of Grace".
Your dark blue cloak billows
to cradle the silence of our sleep
As we sleep these last few greening hours of rest.
Then
You awaken with Your warm breath
and bring us another dawn
Another day –
Like the days of Your kneading the bread,
washing the clothes,
smoothing a teary cheek,
You, our Mother who lived with us, here on earth.
Your silent presence glows
with the fullness of Your humanity
And You love us, know us, forgive us
as only a God can, who has known human bondage.
Hail Mary, full of Grace
Humble Mother
Divine Mother
God the Mother, full of Grace.

WILD MARY

You, with wild hair like tendrils of light flashing across the sky
You, of gentle breath warming the frozen seed
You, of the sigh of release that shakes boulders of granite loose
You, of the peace that cools the earth to sleep
You, by whose feet sun and moon lie down to rest
so they can climb the sky again
You, who birth Grace into creation:
Cradle our unknowing,
Rock us to the symphony of dawn and
the deep single note of evening's dark cello.
Holy Mary
Mother of all
To your silent love cloaking the spheres we listen.

PASSION OF KALI

I WILLED "BE"!
And poured Myself out
to become.
I placed Myself on My pure lotus throne
of holy passion in your loins.
Adoration pure and clean - That is My nature
And your sacred pleasure
when pleasure is bathed in reverence.
Reverence! Reverence! Reverence!
Reverence for My power
igniting the act that creates life out of void
Birth from decay and ooze
And death from magnificent aliveness.
Bow to Me with reverence
in your center of passion, and
step into my realm of holy that is wholeness.
I am the passion
that warms the food you eat
The body you wear
The stars you gaze at
The seed that curls a green leaf out of dark earth.
I am the red-orange passion
that warmed the first thought into Life
And sank the last thought into death's void
In the stillness of Shiva.
I am Kali.
I am the sweet unutterable sound
of the womb of Creation
Rising from depths you cannot follow.

SADHIKA M.

I am the fountain of holiness that flows from you
when you are my altar of passion and purity.
Bow down to Me
and bathe in calm rivulets of surrender,
The peace of gratitude
that ensouls the flesh that opens before Me.
I have set My throne deep within your loins.
So create, and enjoy
And pour yourself out, all of it
in My Holy Name.
Become Me.

AN OFFERING TO MAHĀ LAKSHMI

TO YOU WHO ARE THE richness
at the center of each thing
Throbbing as its mystery;
To You who weave the golden web of life
Yourself in each thread of exquisite beauty
To You who bring forth without measure
from Your brimming abundance
My obeisance, Mother, until the end of time.
Flame of life You are
in every created thing, and the
liquid bliss
pulsing in the secret heart of life.
You are the beauty in my soul and my kindness in action,
the fullness in my heart
Surging over words I search for describing You.
My Mother, my Source, my in-dweller
In whom I rise drop by drop
to the fullness of divine being
Salutations to You again and again.
My own inner beauty
Salutations to You.

"Maha Lakshmi" is a Sanskrit name of the Divine as Mother. Maha Lakshmi is known as the goddess of prosperity, but in Her deeper aspect, She stands for the beauty in creation and for the unstinting outpouring of life force that sustains created things.

RAIN DANCER

RAIN....
Earth's aromas rise
undulating from black soil
Clinging in Her hair
In Her wispy gauze-mist dancing veils
offering tantalizing glimpses of Her beauty.
Loving Her
My wet face receiving Her juice
running down my face
Holding grit between my palms
from touching Her feet.
Rain....
Her eyes soft and gray
And misty
Soft with Her love for me.
A mother loving Her child
A lover gazing into desire.

SNOW BIRD

Snow sculpted a new landscape
in a mad swirling dance
for two days and three nights.
A tiny bird is hopping on top of snow
Too light to even leave a print
looking for just one seed
to stay alive.
Maybe the bird will find a seed
Maybe she will die.
I try to mood-make my consciousness into a love so vast that
it will dance as the snow
Lay itself down fluffy and white
like a quilt of down for the trees
Know the bird's suffering as its own hunger and despair
and still let the tiny one die
so others will sing a stronger earth out of the Dream.
My mind boggles before the immensity of God's love.
A sudden upswelling from the deeps where this love lives
bows my head right to the ground.
Because I cannot love that big
Or that selflessly.

RAGE AND ECSTASY IN MY HEART

The world offers itself in all her wild beauty
her face pockmarked from salty tears
that burned her dusty skin.

In the concrete crack dwells a mystery
that no heart is big enough to contain
So it sprouts green
and joyous
in a trembling haze of hope.

A veiled softness wraps the one felled by a bullet,
The one poisoned brown and dry from the merciless spray,
The one whose bubbling joy is stilled
from the killing muck cruelly poured into its face,
The one whose defeated wings beat no longer,
The one whose pristine womb is bruised
from the grasping fingers of
would-be slave masters.

Yes, all this is a wild beauty with
thorns that will draw blood if you embrace it.
It is the only beauty the world offers
Waiting to be received,
Crying for you to recognize
that a web of heart-breaking love holds
both the slayer and its victim.

If you can imagine
Forgiving with no excusing,
Delighting in
the innocence buried
inside a murderous mind,

If you can be the peace of a mother's love
holding her sleeping child
even as the pain of the world pierces you
Then you have known a drop of a drop
of Her supreme ecstasy.

WHAT SELF?

SITTING, STANDING, looking, feeling...
Your wild ecstatic vibrations keep
brushing against my senses and
I abandon myself to the promise of passion
thinking we will make love.
But what "self"?
Turns out I don't have one.
All that limitless space inside me, all that vibration
Is You at play.
So I am not a lover
but a flimsy shell
of You around You
A wildly colored circle a toddler made on his face
enjoying his crayons.
You drew me so You can revel in discovering
what fun it is to create.
Can anything be more deflating than this?
My ego is a colored smudge on God's face.

ABOUT THE AUTHOR

Sadhika M (pen name) has been a social worker, cabinetmaker, nonprofit executive, corporate consultant, college professor, mobile food vendor and farmer in her unusually diverse life. Sadhika likes to say she crammed 5 lifetimes' worth into this one because she is trying to get it done and go home.

Sadhika's journey as a poet and a spiritual seeker began at the age of 25 with a shattering direct experience of the Divine as an unimaginably powerful, fully conscious radiance - in short, an Infinite Person that was made of love. She thinks of that day as "the day God cooked my goose." Since then, the longing for that Friend, Mother, Lover, Source has been the backdrop of her life. At present, Sadhika lives on her homestead in the rural northeast in the United States. She devotes her time to gardening, writing and deepening her spiritual practice.

These poems are offered to seekers who know what they are looking for, as well as seekers who feel the unease of yearning for something, but do not yet know what that something is. If you are wondering if you are on the way somewhere or lost in the tall weeds, you ight recognize your experiences in my journey and take heart.

We are all on the journey home to the core of our being, but our culture provides no signposts for the journeyer. Every step is a step into the unknown, and those of us who grew up in the western culture have to walk blind. It is scary. For those who know what journey they are on, Sadhika hopes that these poems will reassure them that they are not crazy. Someone else has been in this soup, and came out all right. So far. For those who are looking for something that they cannot yet define, maybe one regular Jane's lived experience will help make the road stand out more clearly from the rabbit trails that dead-end with yet another thing that promised enduring joy but worked only for a while.

www.ingramcontent.com/pod-product-compliance
Lightning Source LLC
Chambersburg PA
CBHW071327040426
42444CB00009B/2101